FROM ONE OF MAYOR KOCH'S
RADIO CALL-IN PROGRAMS
(During the Great Water Shortage)

Koch: "Yes, this is the Mayor."

Woman Caller: "I got trouble with my water."

Koch: "Heh, heh; Madam, all of New York is having trouble with the water shortage."

Woman Caller: "It ain't the shortage I'm worried about. It's more serious than that."

Koch: "What is your problem?"

Woman Caller: "When I turn the water on in my kitchen sink, it's coming out brown. I don't know what to do."

Koch: "Drink seltzer!"

'HOW'M I DOING?'

The Wit and Wisdom of Ed Koch Mayor of New York City

An unauthorized edition
With a foreword by Clive Barnes,
Drama Critic of *The New York Post*.

A JAMES A. BRYANS BOOK

Published by
Dell Publishing Co., Inc.
1 Dag Hammarskjold Plaza
New York, New York 10017

Dell ® TM 681510, Dell Publishing Co., Inc.

ISBN: 0-440-03728-X

Printed in the United States of America

First Dell/Bryans printing—February 1985

This book is dedicated to
The Mayor of the great City of New York,
The Honorable Edward I. Koch,
without whom this volume
would not have been possible.

The Editors

Foreword.

A "Tony" for the Mayor

Politics is today a specialized branch of show business, and if you don't understand that you'll never understand politics. And just as New York City is show business' hub, so the City's mayor tends to be politics' top banana.

Consider Mayor Edward I. Koch. Ed is so much into show business—he is such a consummate actor, with his mobile comedian's face and hair-breadth timing— that when he loudly asks, "How am I doing?" you wonder if he expects a Nielsen rating in reply.

And you have only to see Hizzoner perform in one of those mini-dramatic revue bashes annually devised by the political writers attached to City Hall— The Inner Circle—to realize that when the city gained a mayor, Broadway lost a clown.

The style of the man is a carefully balanced mixture of sherbet and gunpowder, of elfish sweetness and abrasive confrontation. Watch the way he handles hecklers at a public meeting. Watch his dramatic footwork . . . his barbed, unbaited wit, simple but deadly . . . and his St. Joan-like belief in his own saintlinees.

He is the medium-cool media pet, and he knows it. He is fantastic copy, even when repeating himself. Television might have been made for him. His face. when explaining policy, fighting injustice, or expounding good sense, is a picture—a moving picture—of a righteous man in heavy turmoil. His voice rings with honesty, and his eyes shimmer with truth.

The performance is all the more impressive because, whatever it was when he started out, it is today no longer a performance. Stanislavsky would have adored our Ed, because he is now a forthright man acting forthrightly. The message has become the medium.

How is he doing? I know nothing about politics. I just know what I like, and as a dramatic critic, I would rate Ed Koch as terrific. His playing of Ed Koch is the best one man show since Emlyn Williams first played Dickens. I'd recommend him for a special Tony Award— with affection.

Clive Barnes
Drama Critic,
The New York Post

Reprinted by permission
This article originally appeared
in the February 26, 1981 edition
of The New York Post
1981 New York Post

'HOW'M I DOING?'

On Being Mayor
"It's terrific being the Mayor."

On Opposition
Some commentators seem to feel that
Mayor Koch unsheathes his verbal sword too
often, exposing the blade. "I give as good
as I get," Koch says. "I'm not one to turn the
other cheek. Do they think I will be a
punching bag for them? I punch back."

On Public Speaking
Koch feels that his prepared speeches come
out lifeless. He isn't too happy about it.

"I'm a good talker," he says, "but I can't read speeches. It has something to do with eye span. I can't look down and look up."

On Gracie Mansion
The Mayor's first night in Gracie Mansion turned out to be a modicum uncomfortable. The building remained unheated on a very cold day and even colder night. When the Mayor emerged in the morning, he was "chilled in body but not in spirit." He faced his public with his usual confidence: "They can reduce the temperature to zero," he said. "And I'll stay."

On Quick Thinking
The Mayor usually has grapefruit for breakfast. But on the morning of his inauguration, he switched to an apple. "I didn't want to have my shirt squirted with grapefruit juice," he said.

On Coolness of Mind
Asked how it felt to become Mayor of New York, Koch replied, "I was more nervous at my Bar Mitzvah."

On Being Sexy
In a newspaper pool, 84% of the single

women queried voted Mayor Koch as "the most desirable male." Koch, with his usual aplomb, agreed with their choice. "I am the sex symbol," he claimed. "It restores my ego somewhat because Mary Lindsay said I was unattractive and was not sexy. And why shouldn't the Mayor be a sex symbol anyway?"

Ed Koch and The Affair of The Missing Mascot

Archie, a large, friendly mutt who is the mascot of Gracie Mansion, the official Mayoral residence, disappeared one summer morning and Ed Koch was disturbed ("He eats everything. He likes chicken liver.") and offered a $50 reward out of his pocket for the return of Archie, who actually belongs to Koch's chef, Mitchel London.

The next day, Ed Koch interrupted the daily press conference to discuss various theories about his disappearance:

•Had Archie gone in search of romance? "It's possible. This dog was the Jimmy Walker type." (Mayor James J. Walker was a legendary ladies' man.)

•Had he not felt at home? "Dogs are not exactly as rational as people. I'd never run away from Gracie Mansion."

•Had he left to protest working conditions? "Why didn't he just picket?"

•Had he been taken by the Mayor's political enemies?" I don't think politics in New York City has stooped so low as to dognap."

The happy ending to the Archie mystery came a few days later when he was returned by an attendant from a parking lot near the Mansion. While Archie posed at the press conference, the city's chief executive demonstrated the technique of command.

"Sit." (Archie remained standing.)

"Archie! Talk, talk, talk, talk." (Archie was silent.)

"He doesn't want to talk."

After the demonstration, Ed Koch announced that if Archie disappeared again, he wasn't offering a reward.)

On Respect for the Mayor

In his years as an Assemblyman, City Council member and Congressman, Ed Koch always told everyone to call him Ed. But he doesn't any more. When asked why, Koch replied, "All power corrupts."

On Crises

On a call-in show, a woman asked the

Mayor why there was no crisis atmosphere in his administration. Koch quickly replied: "You don't want a hysterical mayor, do you?"

On Weather

There was a snowstorm during the first year of his administration with an aftermath of floods. Koch told the press, "I believe that God is testing me. But what are we going to do when they send locusts?"

On Official Cars

Koch wanted to use a Cadillac limousine for his personal use. It was a car the previous administration had reserved for visiting dignitaries. Mayor Beame had used an old Chrysler. Koch described the car: "It is a deathtrap. A deathmobile." He asked for a vote from the people, and the consensus was clearly for the retention of the Chrysler as the official car. "Okay," said the Mayor. "I'll have the darn car turned into a lifemobile. And the Caddy," he sighed. "will have to await the return of Queen Elizabeth."

On How to End Subway Graffit

In a meeting to find a way to keep graffiti artists out of the city's subway yards, Mayor

Koch suggested letting wild wolves roam the yards. "Wolves have ferocious looks," The Mayor said. "And their sharp, gleaming teeth should be enough to keep young spray paint artists off the trains. Moreover, wolves don't bite."

Asked how he knew, the Mayor quickly responded. "I'm the Mayor. And I know that there is no recorded case of a healthy wolf ever having attacked a human being."

Koch as a Disc Jockey

Although the Mayor often goes on radio to grapple with both the public and reporters, he acted as a radio disc jockey one morning early in his administration. Koch called the show, "The Paul Simon and Ed Koch Show." Mr. Simon was not on the show. "What does that matter," Koch said.

At the end of the show (Koch also played works by Anne Murray), the regular disc jockey, Larry Kenney, gave the Mayor a scarf and purple T-shirt. "If they don't cost over $3 I can take them," the Mayor said. "After my three terms, maybe I'll come back as a disc jockey."

More on the Mayor's Dramatic Ability

"I can't sing and I can't dance, but I do have timing."

On Posterity

The Mayor spends an hour or so every weekend taping what he calls the story of his administration. It's usually done on a tape recorder in his Greenwich Village apartment. "I try to capture the flavor of the week," Koch says. "It can be about anything I thought was the highlight; what happened; if decisions were made; why they were made; how I perceived other people." The Mayor enjoys doing it (he did the same thing when he was district leader, City Councilman and when he was a Congressman. "I enjoy doing it. It's anecdotal, and basically it's amusing because there's so much to be amused by. I have a personality that sees the amusing part of life even in the gloomiest of circumstances. This is not a let's tear-into-'em operation. It's not intended to examine motives. It shows some insight into what's happened. And it shows how I've become educated in office." Although the tapes won't be made public until 1988 (when Koch gives them to Columbia University), he recently broke his rule and disucssed one of them. "The most poignant statement was made to me last summer while I was walking on the boardwalk in Coney Island," the Mayor said. "An elderly woman came

17

up to me and said, 'Mr. Mayor, make it like it was.'

"I thought, 'it never was like you think it was, but I'll try to make it better.' "

On Certain Public Meetings (where the audience was hostile)

"This must have been the way it was when Stalin tried the Jewish doctors."

On Gracie Mansion's Fancy Bathrooms

"Look, I love it. I love opulent bathrooms."

On Being Elected a Congressman

"It was the same when I won the Congressional seat. They considered it a posh, social seat. They said they wouldn't elect this guy from the Bronx, this son of Polish Jews, but they did."

On Being Elected (spoken while introducing his predecessor, Abe Beame)

"Here I am, the 105th mayor introducing the 104th mayor. And you know, the first mayor didn't want to let us in? They wanted to send us, a group of Jewish immigrants, back to Brazil. Did you know that? He must be rolling over in his grave . . . and that's what's so wonderful."

On Life

"I'm having a ball. Who wouldn't? One of the major things in life is never to take yourself too seriously."

On the Yellow Flowered Wallpaper in the Bedroom in Gracie Mansion

"Not my style."

On Liquid Refreshment

A caller-in on one of Mayor Koch's appearances on radio programs complained he was more like a grandmother than a mayor. "I expect you to give City Council members a bowl of chicken soup," to which the Mayor replied, "And what's wrong, I ask you, with chicken soup?"

On His Own Achievement

"You know how I always ask everybody how am I doing? Well, today I asked myself, and the answer was, 'Terrific.' "

On His Disposition

"I am the sort of person who will never get ulcers. Why? Because I say exactly what I think. But I am the sort of person who might give other people ulcers."

What Koch Told the President About Food Stamps

"Get rid of the abuses, but don't take food out of hungry mouths."

On Dolly Parton

"Dolly Parton is no plastic lady."

On Being Pushed by Other Politicians

"I was pushed. I was pushed by the Secretary of the Treasury and by Senator Proxmire. They wanted a labor settlement before approving the fiscal plan. Well, next time the unions are going to find me tougher. Because next time, I won't be pushed."

On Success

"I am living proof that someone from the South Bronx can make it."

On Caring

"I am a man of the people. I am among the people. And I know what they need, what they are demanding. What I'm doing is for the people who live and work in this city. That's all I care about. Because I'm never going to run for something else—other than re-election as Mayor."

On Crime

"New York is <u>not</u> the crime capital of the United States. We're 13th down on the list, according to the FBI index. That means you can go to 12 other cities in the country and be less safe than you would be in New York. Of course, that doesn't help if you are the victim. So we are dealing with it."

On Priorities

"For me promotion of the city's economy is a number one priority. Of course, we have ten number one priorities."

On Welfare

"Who in his right mind <u>wants</u> to live on welfare?"

On Jobs

"We want to build up the city's economy so that private jobs will be available for people who want to work, rather than welfare or maintenance jobs on the government payroll."

On Slogans

"I have developed a slogan. It's long but it's good.

" 'The job of city government is to provide a climate for the creation of jobs and profits in the private sector.' "

On New York for Business

"New York has natural attributes from a business point of view. It's located in a purchasing area of some 20 million people—the people who live here, those who come in to work and those who live just outside. There are very few markets like that in the world. And there are buyers. These are shoppers."

On the Allure of the City

"It's an exciting town. It has vitality. Energy. People like it. It had fallen into disfavor and now it's climbed back into favor. New Yorkers who live here are once again proud of it. People who visit like us. They tell me that all the time."

On Renaming Seventh Avenue, "Fashion Avenue."

"It was not an idea that generated in my little brain. I can't remember who suggested it. It may have been an idea that was 20 years old. But when someone mentioned it to me, I said, 'Let's run with it.' We are striving to make the fashion district better, in a whole host of ways: cleaner, safer, better looking. We want to upgrade it. We are the number one fashion capital in the world and we're going to be number one plus."

On Police Commissioner McGuire

"He was my first appointment and when I brought him out to introduce him to the press, one newsman, in a kind of snide voice, said, 'Mr. Mayor, isn't this part of the regular Irish Mafia syndrome?' The reference was to the fact that police commissioners have traditionally been Irish—although that's not why I chose him. Nevertheless, he is.

"I looked at him and said in a tough tone of voice, 'Bob, you told me you were Jewish!' And he looked at me and said, 'No, I didn't, Mr. Mayor. I just told you I looked Jewish.' "

On Muggers and Mugging

"When I ran for Mayor in 1973 (the Mayor withdrew after a month-and-a-half of campaigning) I went to a Senior Citizen center in the Bronx. I was immediately asked about crime and what we were going to do about it. And I said to these elderly people, 'You know, ladies and gentlemen, crime is terrible. A judge that I know was mugged this week and do you know what he did? He called a press conference and said that mugging would in no way affect his judicial decisions in matters of that kind.' And an elderly lady stood up in the back of the room and said, 'Then mug him again!' "

On the Spirit of New York

"There's an electricity here. And what makes it? The fact that we have more than 150 different races, religious and ethnic groups all living together. Cardinal Cooke has pointed out that Mass is said in New York City in 23 different languages every day of the year. Or you can go to Borough Park and the language you'll hear on the street is Yiddish. Go to Canarsie and see the wonderful, well-cared for homes that the Italian-Americans are famous for—if you want a fig tree, that's the place to look for it. Chinatown, Little Italy. Go to Second Avenue and Seventh Street, there are the Ukranians. Or to Brighton Beach and you have Odessa-by-the-Sea. No other city in the world has that! Like Jacques Brel's marvelous song, 'New York City's alive and well and living on the Hudson.' "

On Chinese Bicycle Sweepers

When Koch was in China he saw the manner in which the streets were kept clean. He admired the bicycle-powered sweepers, and later New York City received a gift of two of them from the Chinese Government. "I'll tell you a story about them," Koch says. "We saw them in Shanghai and they were rather nice. And we're very thankful to the People's Republic of China. But the machines they sent us are not the ones we saw. These are sleeker, better designed, they have chromium on them. They're the American models. Only they don't pick up as much. If you want to do any heavy lifting, these aren't the machines to do it with.

"We are using them, though, and they do good work in a special area. With the walruses in the zoo. And it's very nice! Maybe they could follow the elephants around or something. But we're grateful. I never look a street sweeper—especially when it's a gift—in the mouth."

On Chinese Food

Rumor has it that the Mayor enjoys egg rolls more than bagels. He is allegedly a Chinese food maven. "I go to Chinatown at least once a week, over the weekend. I have about six favorite restaurants and I'm not going to give you a single name because I don't want to stand in line any more than I do now—and I do stand in line like everybody else."

More on Chinese Food

"It's the best buy. You can get away for under $10 . . ."

On Cooking Chinese Food

"I don't know how to cook Chinese."

On Koch Cooking

I do cook about six or eight dinners a year in my apartment. Half in the winter, half in the summer. I have a nice terrace."

On His Winter Menu

"The winter menu is hors d'oeuvres of first rate cheese I get from Murray's Cheese Store—very cheap and very good. Then, I have steaks which I get at the Florence Meat Market—really super. Then I have salad, which I'm an expert at making. The key to it is garlic. And I finish off with either Breyer's or Sedutto's ice cream because both are made in New York City and I buy New York by motto. I generally get burnt almond or chocolate chip—whatever's on sale. And then excellent coffee—which I'm really good at. I use a Chemex, and measure it carefully. Followed by brandy. I happen to like Spanish brandy better than French. It has more of a bouquet. That's my winter menu."

On His Summer Menu

"The summer menu is exactly the same as the

winter menu except for the entree. I cook only when the shad are running and then I make shad for my guests."

On Making Coffee

"I make perfect coffee because I follow the directions perfectly."

On the Secret of Giving Good Dinner Parties

"I invite eight people—never more because that allows you to have a single conversation around the table, as opposed to three or four people talking separately. But the secret to these really good dinners, which start around 7:30 and end about three in the morning, is 11 bottles of wine for eight people. I have found that that <u>always</u> has a wonderful effect."

On Popularity

"I know that I'm popular. A woman summed it up in a very special way on Atlantic Avenue in Brooklyn. 'Gee, I think you're terrific.' So I asked why. She said, 'Because of the way you do what you're doing. It's so easy. There's no pomposity' I think that's true!"

27

On Personal Weaknesses

The Mayor has been asked to define his weaknesses by a number of interviewers. Koch replies, "I'm really not able to answer that. I'm really quite satisfied with myself."

On His Combativeness

Mayor Koch likes to quote Congressman Charles Rangel on Rangel's statement about the Mayor. "You think he's mean to you? He's mean to everybody."

On Labor Unions

"The labor unions make contributions to everybody. They don't care if you're Attila the Hun as long as you do what they want."

On Profanity

Mayor Koch has often campaigned for his friends and associates. When Robert Morgenthau was running for District Attorney of Manhattan some years ago, Koch accompanied him to a street corner rally close to Bloomingdale's. A wild-eyed member of the Progressive Labor Party pushed a megaphone in Koch's ear and cried, "War criminal! War criminal!"

Koch gave him a dirty look and said, bluntly, "F---off!"

The young man was visibly shocked by the Mayor's epithet. "Can I repeat that?" he asked. Koch good-naturedly said, "Sure," and the young man turned to the crowd, and in a loud voice through the megaphone, shouted, "Congressman Koch just told me to f--- off!"

The audience of several hundred people immediately burst into applause, closed in on Koch and began shaking his hand.

On His Prodigious Memory

Mayor Koch is noted for his extraordinary memory. He has phenomenal recall. Not long ago, he ran into Mel Brooks and Anne Bancroft in the world-famous Maxim's restaurant in Paris. Brooks asked Koch if he recalled when they met "in the Village in my brownstone?" Koch remembered. It was in 1962. Koch had decided to run for the Assembly (it turned out to be futile at that particular time) and needed signatures on a petition. As he knocked on the door of the Brooks' brownstone, Koch recalls "a monster dog rushed by" with Brooks and Bancroft in hot pursuit. The Mayor, who didn't know them then, joined in the chase and helped catch their dog. "That's when Annie and I signed your petition," Brooks reminded the Mayor. Koch says, "I didn't say it to them in Paris, but <u>he</u> signed, <u>she</u> didn't. I remember."

On Answering Mail

"I acknowledge every note. You know why I do it? Because people don't believe a mayor sees the mail. They think there's this gigantic maw and shredder at City Hall. When we came in, there were thousands of unanswered letters downstairs. My understanding was that the Beame administration's position was not to answer substantive questions so as not to be on record. Answering my mail is not a fetish. It's purposeful. Besides, it's gracious."

On Slights and Revenge

Mayor Koch is a graduate of NYU Law School. While he was a student, he was upset by what he considered as anti-Semitism by one of his professors. "I remember that the professor told the class that when I went to school, not every son of a shoemaker or butcher or cloakmaker could go."

More than twenty years later, when Koch was in Congress, he was invited to give the convocation speech at a graduation ceremony at the law school. In the audience was the allegedly anti-Semitic professor. Koch pointed the man out and made flattering references to the professor's great ability as a talker. The old professor beamed. "I remember one of his little comments twenty-two years ago," Koch continued, telling the graduates, "when he said to this class of eighty-three people—many of them Jewish, many of them Italian, some of them black—that when he went to school, not every son of a shoemaker, butcher or cloakmaker could go. Well, twenty-two years later that school invited this son of a cloakmaker to come back and give this address."

Koch told a <u>New Yorker</u> writer, "That gave me a great feeling, I must say. I watched his face. It just shrivelled." Koch went on to say that the grandmother of one of the graduates came up to him and took his hand and thanked him for "saying that." Koch said, "For me it was very moving. How much crap do people have to take. And isn't it wonderful to be able to hand it out. I don't forget. I get even."

On His Uncle's Hat Check Concession

When Ed Koch was twelve, he worked in his uncle's hat check concession. "My uncle, who was not such a nice person, sold this hat-check concession to us on terms that were just onerous. People paid to have their hats and coats checked, and we lived on tips. And this was in the Depression—very tough. First they pay to get in. And then they come and we hat-check. It was very demeaning. It was demeaning to ask people, as we did, 'Don't forget the hat-check boys.' That left a trauma, I must say. To live on the largesse of people is something that I consider demeaning. But I was very good at it. I've always been a very hard worker."

Ed Koch's Favorite Words (most used in quotes)

Vile.
Outrageous.
Betrayed.
Richies.
Unforgiveable.
Schmuck.

On Being Tough

"I was doing what was right in a controversial area and being deserted by friends. It made it possible from that point on not to fear."

On Categorizing His Politics

"I'm a sane liberal . . ."

A Promise He Didn't Keep

When he lost (his only loss) in 1962, Koch
said: "I'll never run again. It is a filthy
business."

On Refusing to March in Anti-War Parades Led by Those Who Waved the Viet Cong Flag.

Koch was an early opponent of the Viet Nam
War, but he often refused to march in
peace parades run by those he considered
pro-Soviet, and who "cheered Viet Cong
victories."

"They hated America," he says. "They
were pro-Soviet. I've been there. It's a
terrible society. Everybody wants to leave.
Open the gates. They'll all come out."

On Certain of Bella Abzug's Followers

". . . her savages."

On Reformers and Certain Liberals

"Reformers and liberals never excuse human
frailty. They have absolutes that everybody
has to meet, an absolute test. But that
changes from day to day. That's the point.

It's not 'What did you do yesterday?' No, it's 'What are you doing today?' You may be with them on a hundred issues and then on a single issue you will not be. The others get wiped out. They don't care about that. That is expected. I don't really like them."

On Herman Badillo

Mayor Koch has his share of opponents. One of the most vocal is former Congressman Herman Badillo—who began with the Koch administration as a deputy mayor. Badillo has accused the Koch administration of being "inept." Mayor Koch had a comment on Badillo's accusation. "People who have been fired usually consider their former bosses inept."

On Low Cost Housing

When Koch stunned his liberal followers by opposing low-income high-rise housing in a middle-income community, he was bombarded by leading Democrats—among them, Stanley Geller, a well-known Village Independent Democrat. When Geller beseeched him to change his mind, Koch said that he was certain that the project "will destroy the area." Geller replied, "You can never come out against low-income housing no matter how big the project is." Koch insisted that people will move out of the area if the project came through.

"I don't care if they move," Geller said. "The Jews in Forest Hills have to pay their dues."

Koch paused and then said, "Stanley, I wish I had a town house like you, a pool like you, or kids in private school. Jews are willing to pay their dues. They're just not willing to pay yours."

On Removing the Profit Motive
"When you remove the profit motive, that's what happens. You remove the penalty. There's always someone there to pick up the deficit. Not to hold you accountable. On several occasions, kids have come in from the schools to visit me. This one kid said, 'Why doesn't the city have more athletic equipment, and give us bats and mitts?' I said, 'Wait a minute, kid. You look like the type of kid who has a mitt and bat. Why does government have to give them to you? Why not your parents?' "

On Knee-Jerk Liberals
"I don't believe in half their crap. That government has to become bigger. That

government is better if it does more. It's the New Deal out of the thirties—that government solves all problems. I once believed that. I have contempt for government. I should know. I'm in it."

On Why He Has Sounded Less Liberal as a Mayor Than as a Congressman

"There are two reasons for the change. One is that from Washington the perspective is different from what it is here at home. In Washington, you're removed from the problem of meeting your budget constraints. You're dealing with part of the elephant, the part you like the best. You have this huge elephant that people are feeding. And, I'm not dumping on the Congress. I had the same perspective when I was in Washington. I was doing the same thing they are doing."

On What He Would Do if He Were Still a Congressman

"If I were down there now, I'd be much more conservative fiscally."

On His Advisors

"My cast of characters is whoever is there in the morning."

On Annoying People

"I always like to tweak people if I can, especially if I don't like them. This is something that's really vicious in me."

On Professional Do-Gooders

"The good government groups and social workers destroyed the city for twenty years and they resent bitterly anyone who wants to come in and reassert the balance."

On Getting City Grants From the Federal Government

"You can never know whether you got it just on the merits. But remember, the merits are a judgmental question. There's always the added ingredient—do you have confidence in the person you're dealing with? And—when I needed him, was he there?"

On Duplicity and Artifice

"It is not my habit to employ duplicity or artifice. But I want to make it clear that I am not Billy Budd. Billy Budd was a schmuck."

On Labor Talks

"During the labor talks, did I sometimes have to eat my own rhetoric? The answer is 'Yes.' Did I do it with pleasure? No. Did I do it with an understanding that that's life? Yes."

On Being Honest About Himself

"What you see is what you get."

On Being Jewish

"I'm very conscious of being Jewish."

On Racial Balance in the Public Schools

"Why don't I believe in imposed racial balance in the schools? Because it doesn't work; because it destroys the public school system. People who were sending their kids to the public schools—white, middle-class people—take them out if they can afford it. And the only people who are left there are the poor. Boston being the best illustration."

On Liberal Theory Ignoring Reality

Harlem leader Hilda Stokely told Koch that blacks were not interested in having "our black kids sitting next to your white kids on a bench in the school. What we're interested in is equal schools, equal education." Koch replied, "But Hilda, what you're saying is terrible. You're saying separate but equal, and the Supreme Court says there can't be such a thing as separate but equal." Hilda Stokely answered, "I wouldn't tell a Jew how to bake a bagel," Koch says "she knew more then, and that's what we're learning."

On Everybody Living Together

"Would Chinatown be Chinatown if instead of it being occupied by the Chinese, we made certain that since they're only one percent of the population in the city of New York or even less, on every block there be ninety-nine other people to every one Chinese? It would be ridiculous. Would Little Italy be Little Italy? Is Riverdale a ghetto because it's primarily middle-class Jewish? Ridiculous."

More on Living Together

"I believe that people of like life styles have very little problem in living together. It's people of different life styles who have a problem in living together."

On Minorities in Government

"I have sent everyone a memo that we have so few Hispanics in government. The statistics are deplorable. You have to reach out and seek to bring in blacks and Hispanics."

On Hospitals

Koch was accused of cutting employment

("city hospitals provide jobs for New Yorkers"), when he announced that certain city hospitals would close. He replied, "Hospitals are not for employment purposes. They're for sick people. Hospitals are not supposed to be make-work projects."

Answer to a Request That More Cops Patrol the Chassidic Areas of Brooklyn

"There are only six thousand police on patrol throughout the city on any given day. They can't all be in Borough Park."

Answer to an Associate Who Outlined All the Things an Administration Is Supposed to Accomplish in Services, Budget Stabilization and Development

"Even God couldn't do that."

Answer to a Citizen Who Demanded a Library in His Community

"You want to pay more taxes?"

On Subsidies for College Students

In front of Hunter College, a student asked Koch why the city didn't allow the students to ride half-fare on the subways and busses. The Mayor responded, "Why should we pay for you?" When the student answered that most students couldn't afford the high fare, Koch said, "When I was in school, I worked my way through."

Answer to the Question "Is New York a Sinking Ship?"
"I think of it as a light canoe making its way down river."

On Public Meetings
When too many people shout too many things at Koch's numerous public meetings, he usually says, "Only one problem to a customer."

On Remembering Being Pelted With Eggs at the Meeting of the American Public Health Association
"Y-i-i-chh!"

On the Egg-Throwers
"This is not Iran. Someone has to stand up against these nuts."

On Believing the Egg-Throwing Was an Attempt on His Life
"I thought it was over for me. I was horrified at the moment."

On the Fate of the Captured Egg-Thrower

"I took the bastard to court and he's going to do some time in jail. That's what he deserves. I won't take that from anybody."

On Telling Police Recruits About Being Attacked by Egg-Throwers

"In my mind I didn't give in to it. I wanted to kill 'em. But that thought shouldn't even cross your mind."

On Nasty People in His Audience

"In every community there is a <u>meshugeneh</u>."

On Persistence

If there is any story about Ed Koch which demonstrates his tenacity, it is this one. When he was a Congressman he flew up to New York City to sit on the dais at an important political dinner. He does not like to be late. Hurrying, he crossed Washington Square Park (near his New York apartment) to take the subway uptown. A big man blocked him, Koch says, "He was a big black guy. Every time I tell this story he gets bigger." The man demanded that Koch give him a quarter. Koch refused. The panhandler put up two huge fists. "If you don't give me the twenty five cents, man, I'm gonna beat the hell out of you." Koch thought, "I really should give him a quarter. But no, I'm an officer of the law." He looked the huge panhandler in the eyes. "I'm Congressman Koch," he said. "And I'm going to have you arrested."

Thinking Koch was crazy, the panhandler turned and retreated to other possible victims. Though he was relieved, Koch felt that he must have the man arrested. He couldn't find a cop in the park, so he went after the man himself, who he saw heading up Fifth Avenue. By Eighth-street Koch flagged a police car. "I'm Congressman Koch," he announced to the cops, "and I've just been hustled in the park and I want to have the guy arrested. He tried to extort money from me."

The reluctant cops managed to get the man, and drove him, and Koch, to the Sixth Precinct, where he was booked. After the booking, Koch accompanied the policemen to the Criminal Courts Building where an assistant D.A. told Koch that he was lucky. The man was pleading guilty to harassment, a violation a modicum less than a misdemeanor. Koch insisted on making a statement to the judge. "Your Honor," he began, "I am here because I am angry," and continued for a few minutes concerning visitors to Washington Square Park who are constantly harassed by panhandlers. The judge gave the man a fifty dollar fine. The Legal Aid attorney pleaded that the man should have some time to pay it. The judge gave the man three weeks. As the defendant left the courthouse, Koch recalls, "He smiled at me. I couldn't figure out why, but he smiled."

Koch didn't forget the incident, and in his typical follow-through, contacted the clerk of the court to see if the man paid his fine. When the court didn't answer, Koch wrote again. This time a letter arrived. "I'm sorry our response was delayed. We were hoping he would come in and pay the fine. He did not. We investigated and found that he gave us a false name and address. So we have now issued a warrant for his arrest."

Koch says that he now understands the man's smile. "This is bizarre. They don't know who he is. They don't know where he lives. But they've issued a warrant for his arrest."

The incident caused controversy when it became public. Friends admonished him for chasing a black man who only wanted a quarter. Koch stood his ground.

On Recognition

Not everyone is familiar with the Mayor. On a tour of Queens, the Mayor and his party approach a man, obviously a Greek national, who is a hot dog vendor. The Mayor grabs the startled man by his hand. "Do you know who I am?"

The man remains bewildered. He stares blankly into the Mayor's face and ventures a guess. "From the telephone company?"

It is one of the Mayor's favorite stories.

Street Scenario

The scene is a new shopping center in Brooklyn. Mayor Koch is surprised when an onlooker shouts, "We want John Lindsay."

Koch, (to the crowd): "Everyone who wants John Lindsay back, raise their hands."

(A few hands go up)

Koch, (leaning forward, with his hands on his cheeks forming a megaphone): "DUMMIES!"

On Al D'Amato

"He has the potential of being one of New York's great senators . . ."

Answers to a Reporter's Question on How He Dared to Insult an Audience in Queens by Walking Out on It (Group wouldn't give Koch time to give a two-minute defense on his administration)

"You don't treat me with respect, I walk out. They've got a kangaroo court in there and I don't happen to be a kangaroo."

On Confrontation

"It's the head-on discussion that sets me apart from the others."

On Reading

"I'm not someone—and I regret it—who reads a great deal. I'm talking about outside of government papers which I read a lot. I suppose one of the things I don't have enough of is a historical perspective on what's taking place. Mine is more an educated instinct."

On Values

"I happen to have as many middle-class values as anyone."

On Jackson Heights

"Jackson Heights is the heart of the city. It's a stable community composed of hard-working taxpayers. I absolutely love them. But it would be phony for me to say that, given the choice of living in Manhattan and living in Jackson Heights at a lower rent, I'd pay the higher rent. Manhattan is the most exciting part of an exciting town. But I feel I identify with the people of Jackson Heights."

On the Middle Class

"I am committed to helping the middle class."

On His Early Clients

"I'll tell you why I love the law. Here are a few of my clients in the last year or so (late 1950's): a Village coffeehouse owner who wanted to name names in connection with police payoffs before the New York State Crime Commission; 10 folk singers who were arrested for singing in Washington Square Park; a sculptor who wrote 'for my unborn children' on a note, tied it to a brick and chucked it through a window of the Soviet Embassy when they set off their 50-megaton bomb."

On Wine

"I shouldn't say this, but I prefer Italian wine to the New York State grape."

On Great Leaders

When Mayor Koch was asked by a Jewish

leader of a prominent synagogue (at a meeting at that institution) if he could name one great world leader, the Mayor said, without hesitation, "Anwar el-Sadat."

The audience booed vigorously.

The Mayor sneered, "Aw, shut up," going on to say that "anyone who might be asked to name three of the world's top leaders would have to mention the Egyptian President and probably would not be able to think of the other two."

On Sadat
"I came away feeling that here was a man dedicated to peace."

On Asking the President for Money
"Mr. President, when I was a member of Congress, I used to think in grand design terms. Now, all I think of is a hundred million dollars."

Three Koch Yiddish-isms
(1) "They're making a big tsimmes out of it."

(2) "Stop with your megillah."

(3) "You don't agree? Well, gezinterheidt."

Koch, the True Sagittarian
"I speak to everbody the same way, whether

black, white, or brown and whether
Christian, Jewish or Moslem. I think it's the
height of pandering to speak differently to
different groups of people. To do that, as far
as I'm concerned, is real discrimination,
real polarization. I believe in being truthful
about what I am and who I am. For
example, there are about 7,000 Ukranians
living on the Lower East Side of Manhattan.
When I was in Congress, they were in my
district. In 1969 their leader came to me
and asked me to march in their parade. I
said, "Sure," When I was marching at the
head of the parade, beside the Grand
Marshal, I said to him, 'If this were the Old
Country, this wouldn't be a parade but a
pogrom. And we wouldn't be walking down
Fifth Avenue. I would be running and you
would be runnning after me. But this is not
the Old Country. We have to learn to work
together.' Well, the Grand Marshal agreed
with me, and I think it was because of our
being honest with each other that the
Ukranians became some of my strongest
supporters. All across the country, I came
to be known as the Ukranian Congressman."

On Greeting New Yorkers at Subway Entrances

"I'm Ed Koch. Did you ever hear of me?"

How Ed Koch's Associates Describe His Laugh

"Heh-heh-heh."

Scene in Second Avenue Deli

Manager (to Ed Koch): "Mr. Koch, I'm not going to put anyone at the table next to you, so you can talk confidentially."

Ed Koch: "But you can't deprive a waiter of his living by taking away one of his tables."

On Cars

"I have not owned a car since 1965. I had a 1955 Chrysler. I sold it for fifteen dollars."

On Why He Always Publishes His Net Worth

"How can I go against my conscience? You expect me to do that?"

Answering His Father's Request for Ed's Help in Getting Him a Post Office Job

"But Poppa, how can I do that? It wouldn't be right."

Another Version of the Story of Turning Down His Father's Request for a Job in the Post Office

"My father sold his fur business to his partner, but after six months, he got bored because he's an energetic man. He calls me up; let's see, he must have been around 77 then. He calls me up and says, 'Eddie' —the only one who ever calls me Eddie is my father— 'Eddie,' he says, 'I'm so bored, I have to get a job. You could get me a job in the post office?' I said, 'Papa, you want me to go to jail?' So he says, 'Well, how about OTB?' I said, 'I'd rather go to jail than call Howard Samuels.' "

On Being Blamed for Everything

"So many people want me to be apologetic I'm beginning to refer to myself as Mayor Culpa."

On Judges

"Judges are not sacrosanct. They believe they are above any kind of criticism by the Mayor. They are not. If judges were not to be the subject of criticism and never to be removed and have lifetime posts, God would have made them federal judges."

On a Day in the Life

"My every day is an adventure. I really don't know what's going to happen from now 'till I get home. A mayor's day is exceptional."

On Becoming Mayor

"The only two people who thought I could win were my father and me. There was no one else, and that's the God's honest truth."

On Climbing on the Camel in Egypt

"A reporter said to me, 'We'd like to get you on this camel. We'd like to have a picture of it.' So I'll tell you what went through my mind. You know, there is a symbiosis, a relationship between the press and people in public office. The press has to write stories and people in public office have to get through to the press to get their story across. And so, you have to have a working relationship with people. And I thought to myself, you know, if I get on this camel, I'll come out like Henry Kissinger, with this Arab headdress and I will look silly and maybe even politically I'll hurt myself.

"And then I said to myself, to hell with it. To hell with it! I know I'm just having a good time here. I'm not on any official trip.

I'm a tourist. And it will help that reporter that I be on the camel. I'm going to get on this camel and I'm going to have a good time doing it. I got on the camel. Was that terrible? I don't think so."

When Egyptian Photographers Asked Koch to Pose for Pictures (One New York reporter claimed that Koch on a camel looked like "Lawrence of Astoria.")
"Bring me your toughest camel."

When Village Independent Democrats Didn't Campaign for Him
"How could you vote to nominate me and then refuse to work in the campaign? That's immoral."

On Political Fusion
"Republicans like Lindsay and LaGuardia were minority party candidates and needed fusion to win. I would like to have fusion support, not because I need it, but to change the nature of what we are doing so that people will see my city administration as concerned with the delivery of services in a non-partisan way."

Comment to Throngs of Angry Chassidim Chanting Curses at Koch

"How'm I doing?"

(When an associate criticized the Mayor for saying "bye-bye" to a hostile group, he said, "Saying a bye-bye has a calming influence. Levity defuses tense situations.")

On Political Opposition

When leaders of the club that launched Mayor Koch into politics approved a resolution urging "candidates in addition to the incumbent to run" for Mayor in the forthcoming election, Koch was unperturbed.

"I hope they find one," he said.

On Listening to an Opponent He Was Supposed to Debate

"You're right."

On Discrimination

"My job is to make sure there is no discrimination in any governmental action. I do not believe in preferential treatment and I do not believe in quotas. Is that clear?"

The Word Next to "Realist" the Mayor Uses Most to Describe Himself

"Pragmatist."

On the Number of Policemen in New York

"We'll never have enough cops . . ."

One of Mayor Koch's Favorite Buzzword Verbalizations

"Prioritize."

One of Mayor Koch's Favorite Epithets

"Feh!"

To a Reporter Who Asked What He Said

"I said, 'feh!' "

On a Favorite Food (Caesar Salad)

"I like anchovies."

On His Former Liberal Self

"I used to be, in Congress, a leading liberal. When you're in Congress, you don't have to pay the cost of it, and we gave away the country. Now I go back to Congress, when I testify before committees, and say, 'Mea culpa and you too.' "

On the Environment

When I was in Congress, I had a 100 percent environment record. Now I don't. I think I have more wisdom. I voted in Congress to end all ocean dumping of sludge by 1981. Now that I'm the Mayor, where am I gonna put it? Am I gonna take it home with me at night?"

Favorite Catch Phrases of Mayor Koch as Reported in New York Magazine

1. "Let me sum it up for you . . ."
2. "Think of it . . ."
3. "Let me say . . ."
4. "You'll be interested in knowing . . ."
5. "But you have to understand . . ."
6. "I'll explain it to you . . ."
7. "Do you know what we got out of that?"
8. "Let me tell you the facts . . ."
9. "Do you follow . . ."
10. "Are you following me?"

On What Surprises the Mayor Most About His Job

"I thought I could do more, more quickly. It became very evident that government . . . government is a Hulk."

On Fighting the Monster That is Government

"You gotta keep fighting this monster that sort of wants to overwhelm you and smother

you with rules and regulations and the
protections that are built in to protect
incompetents."

On Keeping a Fighting Spirit

"And I've got to keep fighting against it.
And I will. I will. I'll never lose my energy. I
mean it's just my nature not to lose my
energy."

On Accepting Funds From Washington to Pay Park Workers

After signing the necessary documents, the
Mayor put on a red hard-hat and faced the
federal representative. "Okay, where's the
money?"

On Why There Is Only One TV Camera Present When the Mayor Finds Two Million Extra Dollars

"If this were bad news, we'd have a room
filled with reporters. If we'd lost $2 million,
they'd be around here like ants with honey."

On Refusing to Pose in New York With a Live, Rare Bengal Tiger

"No, the Mayor of New York is not a
coward . . . and the Mayor of New York is
also not a schmuck."

On Medicaid Costs

"If that were lifted from our back . . . we, the City of New York, could lend money to Chrysler."

On the Anger of the Black Community Over the Mayor's Use of the Term "Poverty Pimp"

"Nobody got upset when I called Rabbi Bernard Berman (convicted nursing home operator) a "poverty pimp." I got the term in the first place from Herman Badillo. It was O.K. for him to use but not for me. Anyway, now that I see how people reacted, I've stopped using it."

On Herman Badillo's Statement Linking the Mayor With Mayor Rizzo of Philadelphia and George Wallace

"The polls show that from 62 to 69 percent of the people in this city approve of what I am doing. Is Badillo saying that this huge majority of New Yorkers are racists?"

On the "Koch Style"

"I'm not seeking confrontations or power plays; I'm simply a guy who wants to do a good job and says to the public, 'You've got to help me, but you can't help me by making outrageous demands and taking illegal actions. It's not my intent to be belligerent, but it's not my intention to give in to unfair demands or pressures.' "

On Examining a Suggestion From a Staff Member

"Ach, ridiculous. Thank God I'm the Mayor, not you."

On His Weight

"I have a terrible weight problem. I'm very careful about my weight."

On Energy

"I have an enormous amount of energy. That's genetic. It goes back to my father."

On His 86-Year Old Father

"As strong as a horse."

On the Death of Ho Chi Minh

"Whatever we may think of him . . . and knowing he was a dedicated Communist, we must recognize he was, above all, a patriot, regarded by his countrymen as the George Washington of Viet Nam."

On Deductions

"The fact that we will give a tax break to the

inventor of a hair curler but not a composer of a musical score speaks poorly for the values of our society."

Mayor Koch Takes On the Incredible Hulk

In one of the Hulk comics, a bald mayor appeared. A local paper called the Mayor for his comments about the Hulk. "I see a lot of them running around City Hall. I will round them up and put nets over them."

On the Decriminalization of Marijuana Possession

"By an estimate I have seen, it would cost $79 billion a year to put every pot smoker in jail. And even assuming pot's as vile as its worst critics say, so do you correct that by putting everybody in jail?"

On Mass Transit

"It stinks and it's going to get worse."

On Subways

"The subways are confined spaces. People are afraid. Actual crime in the subway is miniscule compared to crime elsewhere—200 felonies committed in one week in the subway with a total of 3½ million riders every day!

Nevertheless, people are afraid and we're trying to reduce it to the minimum—whatever that is. But there will always be outrages—there are a lot of crazy people running around in any part of the country."

On the Uniqueness of New York

"I do not exaggerate when I say that New York is unique in the history of human kindness. New York is not a problem. New York is a stroke of genius. From its earliest days, this city has been a lifeboat for the homeless, a larder for the hungry, a living library for the intellectually starved, a refuge not only for the oppressed, but also for the creative. New York is and has been the most open city in the world, and that is its greatness and that is why, in large part, it faces monumental problems today. Without question, this city has made mistakes. But our mistakes have been those of the heart. In my administration, I intend to bring the heart and head together."

More on New York

"New York is a place of bounding exuberant diversity . . ."

On New Yorkers Having Left the City

"The weaklings left, they left already, right.

The people who are here recognize this as an extraordinary city. And in fact, as I have said to people, people are coming back. The middle class is coming back to the city. And it's an old line, but I'm going to tell you again. I know that that's true because my sister came back last year."

On His Own Image

CBS newsman John Tesh said to Mayor Koch: "You told a friend and I quote, 'I'm just a dull, colorless person.' "

Koch: "Isn't that true?"

Tesh: "You can't actually believe that."

Koch: "No, I don't."

On Getting Older

"I'm sure I have changed . . . as I have got older. Not necessarily smarter, but maybe a little wiser, and I think we've all grown a little more conservative . . ."

On Personal Philosophy

"I think of myself as a liberal with sanity. I believe in liberalism without dogmatism. I try to understand the problems of others, and find a way to accommodate them without compromising my basic point of view. The liberals are the people you can least count on for personal support when the chips are down. To them, it's 'What have you done for me lately?' Conservatives take a longer view."

On Waste

"The citizens of my city are tired of the waste, mismanagement and abuse that have for too long been endemic in certain social programs, however well-intentioned, and in government operations generally . . ."

On Military Intervention

"It is still legal for the United States to provide military aid to a country to help maintain its internal security. I believe that helping a regime squash an internal rebellion constitutes intervention in the internal affairs of another country. And it must be stopped."

On President Carter's Plan to Pardon Draft Evaders

"Whether one was for the war or opposed to the war—and I fall into the latter category—I believe it's time that we ended a period in the life of this country which is very divisive. And the only way that we can end that divisiveness is to pardon or amnesty these people . . . It is not in any way an attack upon those who responded to our country's call. And I must say candidly— and I served in World War II—that if I had been called to serve during Viet Nam, my makeup is such that I would have gone and fought, because that's the way I would respond even though I was opposed to the war. But that doesn't mean that those who refused to serve should not receive a compassionate reponse from this country. We are now years past the point where the war was ended and most people looking back would say, 'We never should have been in that war in the first place.' "

Answering the Question Whether He Will Ever Run for President

"No, that will be, well, nine more years. I'll be sixty-five years old . . ."

On Pope John Paul

"You don't have to be Roman Catholic to love the Pope."

On Billy Carter

"You're stuck with your relatives. That is true. I happen to have a good brother who I love and respect, and I understand the President's defense of his brother because he has to love, not necessarily respect him. But love him, he's his brother, he's stuck with him."

On City Council President Carol Bellamy
"She's wonderful . . ."

A Prediction That Didn't Come True
"Personally, I believe that Carter will be re-nominated and re-elected . . ."

On Quotas
"I'm against racial and religious quotas, and I think most people are."

On Jerry Brown
"Jerry Brown is not a flake . . ."

On Camels
"I tried to get a camel but these days only the Arabs can afford them . . ."

On the Traffic Problems in Egypt
"They have camel-lock."

On Donkeys (the Mayor rode a donkey in the 1981 Inner Circle show)
"There is a big difference between this donkey and the subway. The donkey's

faster." (The donkey happened to be named "Cruller" and was on loan from the Bronx Zoo.)

On Transportation Decisions Being Made by Albany and the MTA

"I cannot be ignored. I represent New York City."

On Elephants (Mayor Koch wanted the Republican nomination for Mayor as well as the Democratic)

"I wanted to ride an elephant but George Clark (Republican Leader) wouldn't let me yet."

On Movies

According to friends, the thing Mayor Koch likes best about going to the movies is waiting in line. "Because then," he says, "I can talk to the people."

On Being Accused of Always Putting On a Show

"The public enjoys it."

On the Theater

"I don't expect much. Most of what I see in the theater is pretty awful."

On Leadership (and he shakes his fist when he says this)

"Leadership is getting out there and saying this is what we are going to do . . ."

On Being Younger

"When you are young and not as experienced, you are more liberal."

On Being Poor

"I never had a sense of being poor, but I can never remember when I wasn't working."

On the Texture of Life

"If nothing else, I've helped make the Big Apple confident and feisty again, and that's half the battle."

On Being Funny

"I have a sense of humor, but I am not a comedian. I never tell jokes. I do have a good ear for anecdotes and I remember what people say. And I have a good sense of timing as it relates to people."

On Work

"My feeling is, whatever you do, throw yourself into it."

On His Admission That He Spent Too Much Money in Congress

"I would sentence every member of Congress to serve one year as mayor—to teach you a lesson, fellas."

When Asked on a Radio Call-in Show if He Agreed That a Male Policeman and a Female Policeman in the Same Patrol Car Would Lead to Sex

"I disagree."

On His Announcing That He Will Appear on a Number of "Ask Mayor Koch" Radio Programs

"I promise not to read the comics . . ."

On His Personality

"I'm part colorless, and part flamboyant . . ."

On Superpowers

"I'm no miracle worker."

On Budgets

"I'm not able to deliver better services with fewer dollars. It's not possible to do."

On What Jimmy Carter Should Do After Losing to Reagan

"Grow peanuts."

About The Daily News' Evening Edition

"At least it lasted longer than my bike lanes. . ."

When Gas Lines Were Long and Koch Blamed Oil Company Execs

"Five days in the tank will change their attitude— and I'm not talking about the gas tank."

On the Irish

"My name is O'Koch."

On the Puerto Ricans

"Call me Eduardo."

On Andrew Stein

"Oh, I don't like Andrew Stein."

When the City Council Voted Contrary to the Mayor's Wishes

"The first priority is intelligence, and that appears to be missing in this case."

When the Mayor Complained That the Government Provided Only Half the Money for Medicaid in New York While It Gives Mississippi 77 Per Cent, a Pretty Mississippian Delegate to the Democratic Platform Committee Asked the Mayor if He Didn't Like Her State. The Mayor Kissed Her in Front of Everybody.

"Not at all. I love Mississippi."

When Felix Rohaytn Said That a Mild National Recession Could Be an Emergency in New York

"Felix is back in town, and it's nice to have him around with his insights . . ."

When Albany Didn't Pass the Bills Koch Sent Up to Them

"It's the kind of idiocy that makes my blood boil . . ."

(The Times called Koch's statement a "urinative denunciation.")

On House Speaker Fink, Who Actually Didn't Deliver the Bills but Tried

"A mighty oak."

On All Other Albany Figures

"Saplings. That's spelled S-A-P-lings."

On His Immediate Predecessors

"After eight years of charisma and four years of the clubhouse, why not try competence?"

On Being Mayor and Being Uncompromising

"There has got to be a mayor who can make tough decisions and not simply cut the baby in two . . ."

When Asked Before He Left for Egypt How He Was Going to Get to the Airport

"By subway." (He did use the train to the plane.)

On His $291.71 a Month Rent Controlled Apartment. Near Washington Square Park

"I'll have to have some place to go back to after 12 years as Mayor. And the city does not subsidize me. I pay every nickel myself."

On a Possible Opponent From the Liberal Party

"I want to wipe the floor with the Liberal Party candidate—whoever he is."

On Firing Herman Badillo

"This will leave him free to pursue elective office."

On the Movie "Fort Apache"

"I saw it as a fascinating film in terms of excitement, but a racist film in the following way: there was not one Puerto Rican personality that was without some major character defect. But I doubt the film will injure the city's image. People can smell something that is not kosher. This film is not kosher."

On the Subway Fare

"I never said the fare was sacred . . ."

When State Senator John Calandra (a Republican Endorsed by Koch) Said He Would Support a Change in the Primary Date Because He "Owes" the Mayor a "Favor"

"If I were ever to ask John Calandra for help in Albany, it would be help for New York City, not for me."

On Snow Removal

"You know, a snowstorm is like any other natural calamity. You've got to enjoy it even when it hurts."

On the "Legitimate Rights of the Palestinian People"

". . . code phrase for the elimination of Israel."

On American Airlines Leaving New York

"An obscenity!"

"A betrayal!"

". . . like finding out that someone in the C.I.A. is working for the Russians."

On Not Fulfilling All His Campaign Promises

"Oh, who could live up to all those promises!"

On Possible Future Bankruptcy of New York #1

"We're not out of the woods yet."

On Possible Future Bankruptcy of New York #2

"Look, we've come through."

On the Selection of Lazard Freres as MAC's Financial Advisor Without Competitive Bidding

". . . certainly a moral conflict of interest."
(MAC Advisor Felix Rohaytn is a member of the Lazard Freres company.)

Asked if He Was Going to Accuse Rohaytn of Moral Myopia at a Dinner in the MAC Advisor's Honor

". . . look, this is Felix's Bar Mitzvah and you don't say mean things to the Bar Mitvah boy."

On Survival

"When somebody hits me, I hit back."

On Life in New York

"Simple survival is a measure of success."

On Meetings with Anti-NYC Senator Proxmire

"It's like Begin and Sadat. The more you know one another the more you like one another. When the chips are down, he'll come through."

On a Politician He Doesn't Like

"A schmuck."

74

On a Politician He Considers Ineffective
"A nice schmuck."

On Having to Fire People to Save Money
"Am I prepared to bite the bullet and lay off people after everything else has been done? The answer is, 'Yes.' "

On Special Interests
"All the people who normally elect a mayor—the banks, the unions, other special interests—didn't help me, thank God. I owe nothing and can do anything that's decent and helpful to the city."

On Former Congressional Colleagues
"They know I'm never going to lie to them or be careless with figures."

On Some Members of Congress
"Weasels . . ."

On Some New York City Politicians
"Mice . . ."

On Congress
"When I'm asked about Congress, I say it's doing a lousy job. And if I say that, why

shouldn't the constituents around the country say it? Look at this lazy Congress. There's an energy shortage, and we couldn't even get a bill to the floor week after week . . . While I have a high personal regard for the leaders of the House on a personal basis, they're not exactly balls of fire. I've never been asked by the leadership to vote for some position as a matter of party discipline."

On Ronald Reagan's Interest in New York City and Koch

"It's in the interests of the Republican Party to broaden its base."

On Being Chastised for Addressing Both Reagan and Carter Supporters

"I told them all the same thing."

On Being Chastised for Inviting Reagan to Gracie Mansion

"I'm not going to be rude and hurt New York City for partisan reasons. He wanted to be educated in New York City."

On President Ronald Reagan Visiting Gracie Mansion

"He's not going to do any greater damage

76

to us than Carter did. Let's give him a chance."

On Going to the White House to See Reagan

"When he was candidate Reagan he came to Gracie Mansion and we had sort of a continental breakfast. I hope to get better than that at the White House."

The Stuck Elevator Caper

The Mayor got stuck in an elevator for twenty tense minutes with the Police Commissioner and other dignitaries in the Foley Square Court House. Of course, when the elevator finally was fixed the Mayor quipped to the press that his job had its "ups and downs," but what really tickled the Mayor was when the mechanic on the bottom floor trying to get the mechanism functioning yelled up to the elevator operator, "What are you doing up there?" To which the operator responded: "What do you think I'm doing? I'm having lunch with the Mayor."

What Happens to the Mayor When He Goes North of the Bronx

"I get the bends."

On Parties

"I don't like chi-chi parties and fancy restaurants—partly because I hate to pay the bills."

On Enemies

"Crackpots."

On Unemployment

"New York City cannot become the employer of last resort. That's federal responsibility."

On Candor

"I say what I think is right."

On Jerusalem

"If New York City is the Big Apple, you could describe Jersualem as the Apple of God's eye."

On a Tiny Mini-Park in Israel Named after John Lindsay

"Very nice. It's just the right size."

On Being Coaxed to Plant an Olive Tree in Jerusalem

"Now I have a steady supply of olives for my office martinis."

On Begin

"An exceptional man. The American Jewish community is not monolithic. Some people love him. Some criticize him. No one is about to agree with everything he does. I certainly don't."

To Begin

"Your P.R. isn't doing so well in the world press. Maybe you should do something about it."

To Mayor Teddy Kollek of Jerusalem

"You must make sure to retain the entire city. Israel must not bow to any international pressure, including the United Nations where they would even sell their own grandmothers. . ."

On Numbers

"I have to rely on my financial team. I think it's a pretty good one. I never said I was a financial genius."

On Street Grime

"The No. 1 service problem on the public's mind is lousy sanitation service."

On Being Related to Dinah Shore

"On my father's side there is a family in

Philadelphia to which I am related. The Edelstein family told me they were related to Dinah Shore. How, I don't know. I asked her recently and she confirmed the relationship. I haven't seen the Edelsteins in 20 years . . ."

What He Carried in His Suitcase to Give to Fellow Mayors At the U.S. Conference of Mayors in Seattle

Three bags of bagels and lox.

On Keeping His $291.71 Rent Controlled Apartment in Greenwich Village

"Why shouldn't I keep it? How do I know what rents will be like when I leave office?"

On Becoming 55 Years Old

"I can't believe it."

The Word He Uses Most Often to Describe Himself.

"Realist."

On Racists

"There are as many black racists as there are white racists, percentagewise."

On Relieving the Urban League of the Responsibility for Finding Candidates for College Tuitions

(Koch upped the number from 2,000 to 4,000)

> "You can only get these things done if you're willing to stand up and take all the crap that comes from rocking someone's boat."

On Incompetence

> "I hate it. I hate it!"

On Government

> "Government is a swamp into which whole armies get lost."

On the Public School System

> "A disgrace."

His Solution to the Education Crisis in New York

> "Let me hire and fire the principals."

When His Traffic Experts Drew Up a Two-Year Timetable of Studies on the Mayor's Proposed Bicycle Lanes

> "Do it in eight weeks or you're off the payroll."

On His Method of Approach

"I'm very direct to people."

On Experience

"There is nothing that takes the place of experience. You lose the anxiety, the fear of being alone."

On the Future

"I doubt that the next 10 years will have any surprises for me that will be earthshaking."

On His Biggest Dissapointment

"Things do not get done just because the Mayor says, 'Do it.' "

Another Pet Peeve

"Bureaucratic mind."

On Sightseeing in Egypt

"The Egyptians asked what I wanted to see. I said everything Kissinger saw when he was here, and more."

On His Trip to China

"Primary purpose is pleasure, but I'll try to pick up some business for the city."

On Making the Chinese a Business Offer They Couldn't Refuse

". . . but we're not bringing wampum."

On Hospitals

"Nine years from now our hospital policy will be pointed to as our greatest single achievement."

On Criticism

"I won't be intimidated. They call me the Mayatollah!"

On Pushing for an Immediate Referendum on Casino Gambling, Which the Mayor Approves

"If you have a two-year delay, it means a two-year loss of income which means several hundreds of million dollars in revenue . . ."

On Advisors

"You always have to worry about 'yes' people."

On Flavoring Gazpacho

"Use Crazy Jane Lemonade Pepper, if available."

On Personality

"I have a personality that sees the amusing part of life even in the gloomiest of circumstances."

On Learning That Jerry Brown Was Taking Linda Ronstadt to Africa, He Mentioned the Names of All His Female Assistants

"If I were going to Africa, I'd take them all along with me."

On Being Married

"The only times when I feel a wife would be important is when other people I'm entertaining have wives."

On Being Told by General Haig That Hostages Might Not Be Emotionally Ready for a Big New York Parade

"I'm not a doctor. The army's own psychologist said that an outpouring of affection was what they needed. As for General Haig, I hope he'll be a whiz bang as Secretary of State, but as a doctor, he's not so good."

On the New York Ticker Tape Parade for the Hostages

"It will be an outpouring of affection and

respect and love for these American heroes,
because that's what they are."

On Giving Blood

"I hate it, but I do it willingly. But why
aren't the Borough Presidents here? If the
Board of Estimate took my blood, they
should return some."

On Being Told That One-Third of the Blood in Metropolitan Hospitals Had to Be Imported from Europe

"It's a stinking shame that we have to depend
on Europeans to lend us blood."

On Learning That Policemen Get Two Days Off For Donation of Blood

"All I ever got was a cookie and some milk.
But I look forward to it every year. What
would giving blood be without a Lorna
Doone?"

On Being Accused of Racism in Budget Cuts

"How about Mayor Gibson in Newark? He's
a black mayor faced with poverty and he
has to make cuts. But he's not being accused
of racism."

On Allocating Funds

"The city has a big heart but a small checkbook."

Overheard in Conversation with Assistant Diane Coffee

"Diane, would you tell me how you make your Polynesian crab meat spread?"

On Listening to a Doctor Describe the Symptoms of Bubonic Plague as Fever, Pain and the Shakes

"Now why did you do that? I happen to be a hypochondriac. Why did you have to tell me the symptoms?"

On the Death Penalty

"We cheapen the value of human life when we fail to impose the most severe penalty upon criminals who violently take the lives of others."

On Justice

"Sure, swift and tough justice is essential to fairness in the courts and safety in the streets."

On First-Time Offenders

"I believe non-violent first-time offenders should be diverted from our court system."

When a Bill He Favored Was Defeated

"We'll be back. You just can't take 'no' for an answer in this city."

On Being Asked Whether New Yorkers Could Say They Were Better Off Than When He Took Office

"Do you have to steal other people's lines?"

When Italy's Christian Democratic Leader Told the Mayor that New York Was Filthy

"You're absolutely right."

On the Coalition for a Mayoral Choice, a Group Set Up to Find a Candidate to Oppose Koch

"Elitists!"

On Recalling an Unhappy Run-In With a Former Friend, Harlem Congressman Charles Rangel

"Ed," he told me, "you're governing like you want to be a one-term mayor."

"Exactly," I replied. "And that's just why I'm going to be a three-term mayor."

On the Federal Government Encouraging People to Seek New Opportunities in the Sun Belt and to Avoid Cities Like New York

Unprintable.

On New York and Its Relationship to the Rest of the Country

"Those of us who live and work here, we're very lucky. But we don't own this city. It's the premier city——the communications capital, the financial capital——not only of the United States, but the world. And what we want to get across to the rest of the residents of this great country is that almost all of their ancestors came through the Port of New York to settle in Minnesota, to go to Florida or California. And we want a good relationship. I know that it was bad in the past. There was a certain arrogance on the part of New Yorkers which was wrong. There were expenditures made that should not have been made. That's all over. And I believe that this new relationship of affection——affection by New Yorkers for the 49 other states——is recognized. I think that affection is returned. I hope so."

On Senator Proxmire's Dire Predictions for New York

"We refused to accept the idea that New York couldn't be saved."

On Why Carter Lost

"They (the public) were horrified that this country has been drawn through the slime and muck and mud in Iran and that somehow or other our national prestige has evaporated world-wide. And they held the guy at the top responsible."

On Why We Have So Many Transit Problems

"We have 500 Grumman buses that were designed by the government. The government should never design buses."

On Being Chided for Buying Buses That Didn't Work

"I agree with you. But I didn't buy those buses."

When Senator John Heinz (R, Pa.) Questioned Koch About the Feasibility of Giving Any More Money to New York

Koch: "Senator, there is no Berlin wall

around New York. Our poor will have to go someplace. Maybe some place close like Pennsylvania."

Heinz: "Will you give us that statue that says 'Send me your tired, your poor?'"

Koch: "Senator, we may have to sell that statue."

On Accounting
"I do not think it is a science."

Answer to a Woman Who Sent a Letter to the Mayor Suggesting That Paroled Prisoners Not Be Allowed to Return to Stable Neighborhoods.
"You want a Devil's Island?"

On What He Is Going to Do About Transit Problems
"I have asked the Governor for more state assistance and he is resisting me, and I am gonna <u>hock him a chinek</u>. Does everybody know what that means? Drive him crazy!"

On His Predecessor, Abraham Beame
"He was a little over his head."

On His Own Administration
"We wanted to do the least amount of damage as possible."

To Leona Helmsley at the Opening of Her New Hotel

"Go and make money. And hire people and pay taxes."

On Why He Let Comptroller Goldin Use Gracie Mansion for the Comptroller's Birthday Party

"It's my house and he's my friend."

On Being Chided That His Figures That There Are a "Million Senior Citizens" in New York Were Inexact

"We have a million of everything in New York."

On Being Chided for Changing His Mind Too Often

"I believe in the rule of common sense. That means doing what makes most sense when it comes time for you to do it."

On What He Tells Associates Who Exhibit the Same Lack of Reticence as He Sometimes Does

"Shut up."

On Survival

"Never forget, rarely forgive."

On Going to Queens to Help a Black Family That Was Being Picketed for Moving In

"Look, if people can afford a house, you have no right to picket or keep them out."

More on Reagan

"I'm not here to defend Ronald Reagan, but I'll tell you, I like him. He's a man of character."

When the Members of the Metropolitan Transportation Authority Voted Against the Mayor's View on the Fare Raise Because "It Was Unnecessary for the Board to Take Responsibility"

"The last one who said that was Pontius Pilate."

On His Criticism of President Carter's Campaign for Reelection

"When you get my support, you don't get my silence."

On Honesty in Politics

"It happens that intellectual honesty is not the coin of the realm in politics . . ."

On Victory

When Koch entered the primary race,

nobody gave him a chance to win, yet on primary election night, the polls were closed for less than eleven minutes when CBS News cited him as the absolute winner. Koch complained, "I want it to be longer. I want to enjoy it more. It's too early. I refuse to accept victory."

On Recreational Services

When on a radio program Mayor Koch suggested the city might charge fees for some of its now no-charge recreational facilities, reporter Steven Marcus said, "You seem to be suggesting that you would be raising the fees to use tennis courts."

Koch: "That's a very small illustration, all right."

Marcus: "Well, but it's an important illustration because . . ."

Koch: "To you because you probably play tennis."

Marcus: "Well, there are many people in the city who play tennis . . ."

Koch: "Yes."

Marcus: "And use the city's recreational facilities . . ."

Koch: "Yes."

Marcus: "Which have always been free . . ."

Koch: "Try handball. We're not charging."

On Trading

"I wouldn't trade the Big Apple for my own candy bar."

On a Possible Peep Show Tax

"If people are getting pleasure they should pay for it."

On Being Chastised for Sending His Limo to Pick Up His Barber for an Emergency Haircut

"My hair was coming over my eyes. But if I had taken the limousine to go to the barber shop, would anybody have said anything? This way, I could have my haircut in my office, while I was working. But I won't do it again. It was an error which I directed should never occur again."

On the Mayor's Immunity From Ticketing Law

"The Mayor submits himself to the law like any other citizen. The Mayor should not be harrassed. The Mayor should not be immune. I don't think I should be treated any better, but I don't think I should be treated any worse than a citizen is in this city."

On Getting a Ticket for Double Parking After He Began a Downtown Parking Blitz (On why a "ritzy limousine" behind his old Chrysler did not get ticketed)

"The question is whether it is harassment on the officer's part—I don't know—or whether it was stupidity or whether it was simply zeal or what other reasons might exist. I am not peeved. I am not annoyed. I simply cry out for justice."

On Finally Deciding to Pay His Traffic Fine (with his own funds)

"I'm going to pay the ticket. I could have beaten it because the Mayor's car is considered a police vehicle when on official business. But I am going to voluntarily pay the fine because I want these traffic agents to be as tough as they can be. I don't want them in any way to feel that they are not appreciated or that they shouldn't be as zealous as they have been to cost me 35 bucks. (Actually, the mayor was only fined $25.)

Final Words on the Ticket Incident

" 'Justice, justice shalt thou render,' said the Bible. This is New York justice."

On Judges

"Any judge who tacks to the wind to save his or her job ought not to be there in the first place and deserves to be removed at the earliest possible moment."

On the Roots of Crime

"Poverty is not the reason, the paramount reason, the overriding reason why people commit crime."

On Making the Gun Law Tougher

"People are fed up, quite correctly, with crime, and I believe it's my job to do something about it."

On the Nation's Governors and Mayors Who Didn't Want to Have Anything to do With What President Reagan Wanted

"Shortsighted. Let's face the facts. Reagan won the election, and the people want him to try things differently because everything else has failed. Now, if you go against all the cuts and all the changes, you'll end up with no changes that will be helpful, because they'll all get passed. It's easy to be a hair shirt, to go to your constituency and say, 'I fought the good fight. I stood up. I lost, but you can be proud of me.' Meanwhile, you've shafted your constituency because you've refused to be pragmatic."

To the President on Old Folks

"Do you want to be known as the president who closed senior citizen centers?"

On Washington Helping New York City

"There is no answer for us that doesn't include Federal participation. They gave $850 million to Mount St. Helens which has only 26 people. If they gave us the same per capita aid, think of what would happen . . ."

More on Campaigning

"I never take anything for granted. I work my butt off."

In Answer to a Question on How He Ran His City Administration

"Like a very large and quarrelsome Jewish family."

On Negotiating Municipal Labor Disputes (after Jerusalem's Mayor told him he meditated by the Wailing Wall)

"I go down to the Brooklyn Bridge and pray. . ."

On Labor Leaders

"We will never satisfy any labor union leader."

When John C. Dyson, Head of the Power Authority of the State of New York Wanted to Build a Power Plant Over the Mayor's Objections

"John Dyson would have done marvelously in the reign of Marie Antoinette when things were done by fiat."

On Calling for an End to Parole for Prisoners

"When a criminal is in jail for two more years, the people are safe for two more years."

On Being Accused of Concentrating Too Much Effort on Building Hotels and Such in Manhattan

"Who do you think works in those hotels? Overwhelmingly, people who live in the Bronx, Brooklyn, and other boroughs. So it's understandable that private dollars will go into the area where they'll make the most money. It's their dollars."

On Budget Cuts

"I have a billion dollars less each year than

my predecessors who were heading the city into bankruptcy. I don't have more cops, but I am getting more out of each cop. For 30 years, New York mayors have been trying to get two-man garbage trucks. I'm the one who got them."

On Victims of Crime

"I believe that city government has an obligation to assist crime victims by lessening the inconvenience, cost and trauma imposed on them through crime. In studying the criminal justice system over the years, I have been dismayed by the treatment accorded the victims of crimes. No one tells them what is happening . . . they have no one to provide them with assistance, while the defendant has a lawyer . . ."

On Broadcasting Names of Those Convicted of Patronizing Prostitutes

"We're going to call it the John Hour."

On Reporter Jack Newfield's Accusation That Koch Is Ignoring the Poor

"Now, there are some people who don't like the middle class. Newfield, although he happens to be rich—at least, his wife is—they don't like the middle class. They would like to lionize the poor. I was poor. I don't have to lionize the poor. I have to provide services for the poor and try to get them into the middle class."

On Reporter Jack Newfield's Criticism of the Job Koch Is Doing

"He's not a reporter. He's a journalist with a point of view. And his point of view today is 'get Koch.' That's okay with me."

On a Mayor's Job

"A mayor has to do all of those things within the constraints of the dollars that he has available."

Yet Another Favorite Way the Mayor Describes Himself

"Not an ideologue."

On Discrimination

"There are . . . people who believe that you have a guilt complex, that somehow or other you have to pander or provide preferential treatment for blacks and Hispanics. I think that is discrimination to them. I accept them as equals; equal before the law and equal before the government."

When Minorities Occasionally Complain That They Don't Have the Commissionerships They Would Like to Have

"What does that mean? The Parks Commission is occupied by Gordon Davis, who happens to be black. That used to be considered one of those socialite positions. Goo-goos got that; rich people got that. There is a black commissioner who now has that department and is doing the best job that that agency ever had."

On Getting Booed Before a Crowd

"The fact is that you can get a crowd to turn on any speaker if you bring in 20 or 30 people."

On Being Refused by the Reagan Administration to Restore $122 Million in Mass Transit Funds

"In Washington it takes three to tango—the President, the Senate and the House. We're asking them to dance."

On Telling Problems of New York City to Congress

"Do you know another city in the world that spills its guts before the whole country this way?"

On the Battle of the Bulge

Mayor Koch, who hits the scales somewhere around 200 made a bet with Queens Borough President Donald Manes to see which one of them could lose more weight in one week. Manes refused to tell reporters his weight, but estimates ran in the area of 220 or 225. To insure his victory, Manes sent a fifteen pound box of chocolates to Koch who admits to a sweet tooth. The Mayor was the model of resistance. He spurned the luscious chocolates and immediately dispatched a fresh bagel heavy with cream cheese to Borough President Manes (known throughout his domain as a bagel fancier). Manes was a paragon of self-control. He gave the bagel away.

The weigh-in was scheduled to take place at City Hall, but it never happened. Manes was called to Washington on business on the arranged day. They spoke on the telephone, and the Mayor conceded. As loser, he invited the Borough President to dinner at a Queens restaurant, announcing: "I concede. Tubby wins because he has more to lose. Dinner in Queens is being planned. Enough already."

On "Flue" Season at City Hall

Mayor Koch wanted to save energy by

burning wood in the City Hall fireplaces. Peeking up the flue of one of the long-unused fireplaces, Koch quipped that if the chimney is eventually cleared, he will have no problem fueling the fire because "there's plenty of deadwood in city government." Koch accused previous mayors for clogging up the fireplaces. "They were blocked up," he said, "in prior administrations that didn't believe in fireplaces." The Mayor reminded onlookers that Fiorello Laguardia burned cannel coal in the fireplace in his office. When someone chastised Mayor Koch for wanting to chop down trees, he smiled. "I have no intention of chopping down any cherry trees (it was on Washington's Birthday.) All the wood will come from trees pruned or felled by the Parks Department."

Two Comments by Mayor Koch on Hearing That Council President Bellamy Suggested Surplus City Funds Be Used to Keep Subway Fare at 60 Cents

1. "Has she found trees that grow money?"
2. "Maybe she's looking for a cheap headline."

On Money for Policemen

When the Patrolman's Benevolent Association planned to face down the Mayor with a high-powered lawyer, he responded with conviction. "There is no money here. They can bring Godzilla here and there won't be any."

On Possible Opponents in the Next Mayoral Race

"Maybe one of them will have the courage to run against me . . ."

On Politicians Who Make Promises to Israel and Don't Keep Them

"They'll rot in hell."

On Corruption

Corruption appears to be pervasive in our society. I am thinking not simply of the public office-holder who betrays his trust . . . What also troubles me is the corruption of our ordinary citizens. I am thinking of the children who learn from their parents to cheat the storekeeper, the telephone company and the government. I am thinking of corporations who, in turn, cheat the consumer, bribe officials, and do not level with their stock-holders. We see evidence of this corruption daily in the sale of shoddy merchandise, tax fraud performed openly and without remorse.

Medicaid charged for services not rendered, the elderly ripped off by nursing home operators, just to cite a few examples . . . We ought to consider corruption in the same class as that of a physical assault upon an individual . . . I am equally persuaded that the white collar criminal, the corruptor, will be deterred and reformed if he or she serves just 30 days behind bars."

Speaking as Guest of Honor at the New Dramatists Guild

"There aren't many people who enjoy their work. The people in the theater——and I——do!"

When Told He Was the Only "Non-Theatrical" Person to Be Honored by the New Dramatists

"It's clear to me that you are not familiar with my resume."

What the Mayor Calls Gracie Mansion

"My house in the country."

On the Tenancy of Gracie Mansion

"I like it here. It's a nice place and I'm not leaving. In the next several months, I'll be negotiating with my constituents to extend my lease."

On His Second Inauguration

"What a great way to start the year . . ."

To Naysayers on N.Y.C.'s Chances During the Crunch of '81-'82

"This is a city of winners and we're not stepping aside for anybody."

Some Time After Saying New York City Was a "Long Distance Runner and All We Have to Do Is Hold the Line."

"A year ago the wind was at our back. Now it is against us."

On Running for Governor

"A fate worse than death."

On Reconsidering His Statement on Running for Governor

"I haven't put a lock on the door."

On Being Reminded That He Pledged At the Western Wall In Jerusalem Never to Seek An Office Higher Than the Mayorality

"That was a pledge between God and me—not with you and me. If I were to take an action God would consider violative, he would punish me."

Recalling the Roosevelt/La Guardia Era

"I'm not saying that those were the good old days, when in fact they were some of the worst of days. But nonetheless, they were days of hope and spirit and understanding and communication between an American President and the cities of America."

On Discovering the N.Y. Post Wanted To Draft Him for Governor Through a Coupon Contest

"I will not rely on either coupons or polls."

Giving Advice to Democrats

"Stop being a party of the poor! We're not getting across the message that we're not only for the poor, but also for the middle class."

On the General Assembly of the U.N.
(After some anti-Israel decisions)

"A cesspool."

On Changing the Inscription From Isaiah ("Beat swords into plowshares") On Wall At City Park Across From the U.N. Building

"I am going to add a reference that shows hypocrisy, immorality and cowardice."

Where the New Inscription Will Come From

"So now I'm reading the Bible."

When Pravda Accused Him of Currying Favor With the "Zionist Lobby" Over the Inscription Change Brouhaha

"Those red nuts."

More Intense Comment About the Russians

"I don't like them and they don't like me, and that's terrific!"

More About Russians

"What is particularly gratifying is that the Soviet Union has to take note of what I've said."

On Local Criticism About His Concern For the U.N. When He Should Be Concentrating on City Affairs

"The Mayor of New York is not just a city man. Just because I'm concerned about the MTA doesn't mean I shouldn't be concerned about the U.N."

On Finally Deciding Against Changing the Inscription On the Wall

"I wouldn't call it backing down."

On Being Told He's Talked of Nothing Else For Ten Days

"I have made my point by talking so much."

Asked What He Would Have Added To the Inscription If He Had Decided to Change It

"Woe to those who call evil good and good evil."

On Being Told That He Is Considered Impatient

"Baloney."

On Rural America

"You have to drive 20 miles to buy a gingham dress or a Sears Roebuck suit. This rural America thing, I'm telling you, it's a joke."

On Being Told Of Reagan's Budget Cuts Which Would Cost New York City $720 Million.

"Do you want me to frighten people today or just alert them?"

To a State Department Official About His Planned Visit to American Troops in Lebanon.

"Ready or not, here I come."

Answering the Question as to Why Americans in Lebanon or the Lebanese Would Want to See Him

"Wouldn't they want to meet with an American who can bring them news of New York City?"

To Reporters on the Same Question

"I'm a simple little mayor of a city. I'm invited now to meet with the President of Lebanon. Isn't that nice?"

When a Bowery Derelict is Puzzled by Koch's Visit and Offer of Help

"Please sir, I've got money for food and clothes. I want to help you. Don't you know who I am?"

On Realizing that a Great Number of Derelicts are More Disturbed Than Alcoholic

"These people do not live on the streets because they're on their uppers. They are there because they are deranged."

On Being Told the Law Doesn't Allow a "Deranged" Person to be Helped Unless a Psychiatrist Certifies that the Person is a Real Danger to Himself

"Then I say, the law is an ass." (quoting Mr.

Bumble in Dickens' OLIVER TWIST). "We can't bring them in or help them unless they're killing someone with a knife."

On Being Told That He Must Join the American Federation of Television and Radio Artists (AFTRA) (Koch has appeared on many TV shows including the soap opera "All My Children" and the movie "The Muppets Take Manhattan") Even though He Asks Producers to Make Donations to the City in Lieu of Fees for His Appearances.

"The price of fame is high."

On His Support of Israel

"Regarding the line that the American Jewish community is part of some Israeli lobby—well, so what? Why shouldn't we defend Israel? What should we do; go to the gas chambers silently?"

On the Middle Class

"I want the middle class to know they have a friend in City Hall, that when people mocked them in the sixties, they were wrong. The middle class was right. Honesty, industriousness, all of it."

On Mayordom

"A Mayor can be a downer or an upper. I think I'm an upper."

On Loving Mr. Apple

"I've become identified with New York and I think people like me, and they like New York."

On the Complaint That People are Leaving New York

". . . and they're coming back. How do I know? My sister came back two years ago."

On Being Told About the Crime, Dirt and Inconvenience of New York

"Have you ever lived in the suburbs? I haven't, but I've talked to people who have, and it's sterile. It's nothing. It's wasting your life."

On Assassination

"When George Moscone, the mayor of San Francisco was killed, I was asked for my reaction. It shook me because Moscone wasn't killed by a stranger; he was killed by somebody he knew who had access to his office. The point is you can have all the security in the world but you still can't protect yourself."

On Fate

"I happen to believe in the doctrine of
<u>beshert</u>, which means 'God Ordains.' Your
life is laid out, predestined. Obviously you're
not supposed to make it easy for those who
want to dispose of you. You don't throw
yourself in front of a train."

On the Sixties as a Repudiation Of the Mayor's Beliefs

"What happened in the 60s was that the
value of integrity and hard work and
industriousness no longer counted, were no
longer perceived as worthy of reward."

On His Boyhood Idea of Manhattan

". . . when I was growing up, Manhattan was
another planet."

On His Frightening View of Genocide

"Every country is capable of genocide."

On Lord Carrington, the British Foreign Minister Who Claimed the PLO wasn't Involved in Terrorism

". . . a schmuck."

On Loyalty

"I want to say it only once. These are my

loyalties: the country, the city, then Israel—in that order."

On the Alleged Jewish Control of the Media

"Anyone who says the media are controlled by Jews is meshugeneh!" (crazy)

On Some National Figures as Possible Anti-Semites

JESSE JACKSON: "I believe that Jackson has engaged in anti-Semitic remarks, and besides, he went to Lebanon and kissed Arafat on the cheek, and gave terrorism his blessing."

RONALD REAGAN: "I happen to believe Ronald Reagan is very sympathetic to the Jews."

RICHARD NIXON: His Watergate comments were filled with anti-Semitic slurs."

GERALD FORD: "Ford was always very good on Israel."

JIMMY CARTER: "Carter, though, was never any good on Israel but I cannot say he's anti-Semitic."

JESSE HELMS: ". . . Jesse Helms may hate Jews, but he loves Israel."

BILLY CARTER ". . . clearly anti-Semitic. What do you want from a wacko?"

On His Own Puzzling Character

"People have such a hard time figuring me out."

On Political Loyalties

"My loyalties are to the Democratic party."

On Taking Care of the Bastards

"I believe if someone kicks you, it should not be with impunity."

On Being an "Actor"

"I _can_ demolish an opponent in one line, but that isn't the same thing as winning over the state legislature or Medicaid or pulling New York City out of bankruptcy. If I'm an actor, so be it; but don't think it hasn't been good and useful for the city."

On Being Told that Nixon, too, was Considered a "Consummate Actor"

"Nixon! He's a phony. I'm not. My performance is not dishonest. His always was."

On Spiro Agnew

"Agnew, though, I can describe as only 'spittle.' I mean Agnew is so far beneath contempt, he isn't a fit subject for discussion."

On Accusations of His Homosexuality

"No, I'm not a homosexual, but if I were, I hope I'd have the courage to say so, because I happen to believe there's nothing wrong with people who are homosexual."

On Being Called a "Confirmed Bachelor"

"I have not in any way taken a political vow that in order to do my duties, I foreclose marriage."

On His Mental Prowess

I've got a good intellect, not a super intellect. I'm no genius, just a good intellect."

On Being Told Midwesterners Might be put off by His Colorful Language

"Midwesterners are just like anybody from the lower East Side, on the issue of my colorful language. What's wrong with the word 'schmuck' anyway?"

More on Middle Class Values

"I value the middle class ethic because I am middle class."

On Conspiracy

"I don't believe in conspiracy theories. I really believe that Oswald killed Kennedy."

On His Statements about Black Anti-Semitism

"I still believe there are lots of blacks in leadership positions who are anti-Semitic."

On Being Reminded He Once Called Bella Abzug a "Savage"

"I don't remember saying that, but I wouldn't retract it if I did."

On the Sixties Radicals

"The kids went to the best schools and ultimately decided that what they wanted to do was destroy society; I don't know what happened to the kids' brains—whether it's a screw loose or a question of education. In a way, it's like what my mother used to tell my brother: 'You should have a kid like you. God will punish you!' "

In Response to the Many Accusations of his Alleged Narcissism

"Sure I am. A little bit."

On Great Restaurants

Once I went to Lutece and I was very upset. I almost always pay for my own meals, but that time I was invited. I had a wonderful sounding dish and it turned out to be Swedish meatballs. I said to myself. 'Jesus Christ. I come to Lutece, I end up with Swedish meatballs!' "

On Being Told Subway Graffiti was an Indigenous Art Form

"Bullshit. Bullshit twice!"

On Making it Tough for the Criminal

"I want to release the names of juvenile or adolescent felons. The law prohibits it now, but I think society should have a sense of public disdain. People should have to live with their criminal past."

On the Mafia

"Yes, Virginia. There is a Mafia."

On His National Influence

". . . when people talk about New York City, they talk about me."

On Being Asked if He Would Buy All the Copies of Playboy With His Derogatory Remarks on Rural America

"If I could afford it, yes."

On the New York State Liquor Authority's Ban on Patrons Carrying Their Own Wine into Restaurants Without Liquor Licenses (including restaurants the Mayor patronizes)

"It's archaic, it's arcane, it's stupid. It'll raise the price of a dinner. You like to get a little bargain now and then. I mean, that's what life is all about."

On His Virtues

"I'm not overly humble."

On Greeting Guests for Dinner at Gracie Mansion

"There are no place cards, sit where you want but not with the person you came with."

On Viewing a Short Film About Himself in Which the Narrator Praises the Mayor's Guts, Style and Vision

"Not bad . . ."

On Criticism That He'd Been Insensitive to Minorities in Making Appointments

"If I had wanted to buy peace, I could have bought racial peace. But that's not my style."

On Denying That He Was a Political Maneuverer

"The coin of the political realm is to convey to somebody that what they wanted they got, even though they did not. That's not me."

On Speaking Without Forked Tongue

"Everytime you say what's on your mind you're apt to make an enemy."

On His Generosity of Spirit

"I don't get ulcers—I give them."

On Coming Out to a Heliport to Greet President Reagan on a Visit to New York in a Rainstorm and Having the President Say, "You Didn't Have to Come Out in the Rain"

"I'm like the postman."

Rumination Number 362-A on Losing the Gubernatorial Race

"I wasn't depressed after losing the governorship. I was sad. There's a difference."

On Walter Mondale

"He wants to be loved. That's wrong. A politician shouldn't want that. Being loved is a bonus that comes. But you shouldn't want it."

On the Dearth of Good News Coverage by the Networks

"That's not as sexy as talking about race relations and showing some mob scene."

On Giving a Tiffany Crystal Seal to Zhao Ziyang, Prime Minister of China

"Turn it around. You're holding it backwards."

Asked Why He Was Serving Zhao Ziyang Marinated Scallops and Chicken Florentine Instead of the Authentic American Beef Stew He Promised

"I looked into the wrong pot."

On Diana Ross Giving the City a Check for $250,000 for Renovation of a Children's Playground

"Thanks."

On His Being "Mr. Sang-Froid."

"My equanimity in office comes from the fact that I have always tried to tell the whole story, warts and all."

On What He's Made Certain Officials Do

President Carter: "Turn gray."

Congressman Charles Rangel: "Sweat."

Former Deputy Mayor Herman Badillo: "Twitch."

Carol Bellamy: "Cry."

On Former Governor Carey's Wife Evangeline Telling Him How Active She'd Been in Jewish Causes

"Every time she sees me she has this button in her brain that goes off and she spews out what she thinks a Jew wants to hear."

On Why He Was One Of the First People To Back Carter Against Teddy Kennedy.

"Teddy thinks my name is Fred."

On Criticism of His Accepting Campaign Donations From a Law Firm That Represents South Africa

"Don't they have a right as lawyers to represent criminals?"

On Getting Publicity for His Book

"I love it! When I think of the fact that if

my most hostile critics had not sensationalized
my book by obtaining it in advance galleys
and publishing small parts of it, not
substantive parts, just the parts they
thought titillate—why, it would have
taken weeks before it became a Number One
bestseller!"

On Barbara Walters Asking Him if it was "Normal" to be a 58-Year-Old Bachelor

"You've been divorced haven't you? Is that
normal? Does it affect your sexuality? Well, it
doesn't affect mine, either."

On Being Asked, if, When in Rome, He Planned to Give a Copy of His Book "Mayor" to the Pope

"That would be presumptuous. I will give it
to his aide, and then, if he wants to give it
to His Holiness, I would be delighted."

On the Book's Negative Reviewers

"The anger at the book comes from the fact
they didn't write it. These are people who are
envious."

On Suggestions That The Book Might Impair His Ability to Function in Office

"I would have written it even if I believed it would do me damage, because I wanted to do something that would show how government works."

On How Much He'll Make From the Book

"I hope a fortune."

On the Possibility of Having a Lot of Money From the Book Changing His Habits

"A fortune is whatever is required to continue the modest lifestyle I lead."

On the Amazement of Many People That He Could Actually Write a Book

"I think lots of people think I'm not as bright as I think I am."

On His Lack of Modesty Concerning the Book

"I'm not Mr. Humble Pie."

On the Possibility of a Second Book

"I wouldn't climb Mt. Everest twice. Why should I try to write a second book? It probably would be a failure."

On Meeting With the Pope in Rome

"We hit it off beautifully."

On the Communist Mayor of Rome

"He is a rather charming man, although he is not of a party I have the highest regard for."

To Checkpoint Charlie (separating East Berlin from West Berlin) Border Guards Who Kept Snapping His Picture.

"I'm here. It's me. It's me."

On Kissing the Stone Portal Remnant of a Berlin Synagogue Destroyed by the Nazis

"I was compelled to kiss it because I was overwhelmed by the thought that barbarians could have destroyed a place of worship."

On Talking to Reporters After His European Trip

"Did you miss me?" (The mayor ignored the reporter who quipped: "Were you away?")

On Telling the Press That the Crime Rate is Way Down

"If crime goes up, you're going to blame us. So if crimes goes down, give us a little credit."

Singing a Song Written by His Speechwriter Clark Whelton

"I would like the universe to get down on its knees/and say 'Edward whatever you please/ It's O.K. even if it's reee-dic-u-lous!' "

On Being Told Of a "Terrific" Restaurant With a Hundred Dollars For Two Tariff—Before Tips, Tax, or Drinks

"Oh, come on. I can't afford that?"

On Being Asked if He Still Cooks

"I cooked much more before I became Mayor."

A Cook's Confession

"I don't know much about vegetables."

On How to Run a Dinner Party

"I don't believe the host should leave the room for more than five minutes at a time."

Mayor Koch's Secret Super Dessert Revealed:

"For dessert I serve Breyer's ice cream. You get a half gallon for less than two dollars and it's very good ice cream. The fancy schmancy brands cost two dollars a cone. I love Breyer's butter pecan and chocolate tidbits and Armagnac. That really was wonderful. Everybody loved it."

On Being Desperate for Fat

"I love fat meat and fat fish."

On Being Asked About the Cholesterol Content of Fat Fish and Meat

"My cholesterol count isn't affected by them—even if I believed in cholesterol."

On Discussing a Very Popular Restaurant

"You have to make reservations unless you happen to be the mayor."

On His Popularity With Restaurant Owners

"My picture's in the window or over the cash registers in all my favorite places."

On the American Dream

"New York City is the city of the 80's and

127

beyond, the city that will not allow the American dream to go down in defeat. Because New York City is more than the American dream. New York City is the city that dreamed America . . ."